SPECIAL
CEREMONIES

Feasts and Fasting

Cath Senker

HODDER
Wayland
an imprint of Hodder Children's Books

SPECIAL CEREMONIES

Feasts and Fasting

This book is based on the original title *Feasts and Fasting* by Kerena Marchant, in the *Ceremonies and Celebrations* series, published in 2000 by Hodder Wayland

This differentiated text version is by Cath Senker, published in Great Britain in 2005 by Hodder Wayland, an imprint of Hodder Children's Books.

Original designer: Tim Mayer
Layout for this edition: Jane Hawkins

Consultants:
Working Group on Sikhs and Education (WORKSE);
Rasamandala Das;
Jane Clements, The Council of Christians and Jews;
Jonathan Gorsky, The Council of Christians and Jews;
Dr Fatma Amer, The London Central Mosque;
The Clear Vision Trust.

Picture acknowledgements:
Circa Picture Library 6, 18 (William Holtby);
Hutchison Library 1 (Nigel Howard), 8 (Nigel Howard) 21 (Juliet Highet), 26 (Patricio Goycoolea), 27 (Liba Taylor), 29 (Nigel Howard); Panos Pictures 28 (Daniel O'Leary); Peter Sanders 4, 14, 17; TRIP 5 (H. Rogers), 7 (H. Rogers), 9 (H. Rogers), 10 (S. Shapiro), 1 (H Rogers), 12 (A. Tovy), 13 (A.Tovy), 1 (C.Rennie), 16 (H. Rogers), 19 (H. Rogers), 20 (Dinodia), 22 (H. Rogers), 23 (H. Rogers), 24 (H. Rogers), 25 (B Dhanjal).

British Library Cataloguing in Publication Data
Senker, Cath
Feasts and Fasting. - Differentiated ed. - (Special Ceremonies)
1. Fasts and feasts - Juvenile literature
I. Title II. Marchant, Kerena
203.6

ISBN 0 7502 4652 9

Printed in China

Hodder Children's Books
A division of Hodder Headline Limited
338 Euston Road, London NW1 3BH

Contents

Food and Faith

Food and drink are vital in our lives, and play an important role in religion too. Most religions have rules about which foods to eat and those to avoid. On religious holidays, people may eat special dishes and enjoy feasts. On other occasions, they might go without food so that they have more time to think about their religious beliefs.

Fasting

There are different reasons for fasting. Sometimes people fast before making an important promise or starting a new way of life. They may fast to make them feel closer to God. Sikhs and Buddhists do not encourage this custom. They do not believe that it helps people to develop religious faith.

▲ Hindu *sadhus* (holy men) fast to strengthen their religious beliefs.

Feasting

People of many religions hold feasts on special occasions, such as the birthday of a religious leader. Often there are particular foods to help people to remember the events they are celebrating. A feast is usually on a holiday so family and friends can get together. Plenty of food is provided for everyone. The dishes might be more expensive than normal food and take a longer time to prepare.

Food customs

Most religions have ideas about what you should eat or drink. Christians may eat what they want most of the time, except during Lent. Many Jewish people eat only *kosher* food. Their meat is prepared in a special way. Muslims eat *halal* meat, which is also prepared in a special way. Sikhs and Hindus mostly eat vegetarian food. Some Sikhs and Hindus choose not to drink alcohol because they believe it harms the body.

▲ Sikh vegetarian dishes: spinach and cheese; dhal (lentils); rice; roti (bread), and raita (yogurt and cucumber).

The Christian Tradition

Lent and Easter

Lent is a period of 40 weekdays when Christians prepare for Easter. At Easter they remember how Jesus died and rose from the dead. During Lent, many Christians give up something they enjoy to help them to strengthen their faith.

Members of the Orthodox Church keep Lent very strictly. They give up both meat and dairy products. Western Christians often choose to give up a luxury food, such as chocolate. Some people go to Bible studies classes to learn how they can become better Christians.

◀ People make pancakes from milk, eggs and flour. They sweeten them with sugar and lemon juice.

The day before Lent is Shrove Tuesday, when people make pancakes. This comes from the tradition of using up all the fatty foods in the home before the fasting season of Lent.

The last Friday of Lent is Good Friday. Christians remember how Jesus died on the cross.

HOLY BOOK

Jesus taught that people should keep their fasting a secret rather than showing off that they were doing it.

'...when you fast, put oil on your head and wash your face so that it will not be obvious to men that you are fasting, but only to your Father, who is unseen; and your Father, who sees what is done in secret, will reward you.'

From *The Bible: Matthew 6:1–6*

◀ Christians in Greece parading religious icons around the streets on Good Friday.

▲ Greek Orthodox Christians call the first day of Lent Clean Monday. On this day, they eat meals that do not contain meat or any other animal products.

Easter Sunday

On Easter Sunday, people remember how Christ rose from the dead. It is a day of great celebration and feasting. Around the world, Christians eat different foods. Many people eat lamb in memory of the lamb Jesus ate at the last meal before his death. Orthodox Christians have a rich Easter feast with all the foods they were forbidden to eat during Lent.

KATIYAH'S STORY

'I'm 12, and I'm from a Greek Orthodox family. After the Easter Sunday service at midnight we go home for a meal of Easter eggs – eggs that are dyed red. Later that day we eat cakes and breads. In the evening we eat a meal of lamb stuffed with almonds and raisins.'

Here are eggs dyed red, and modern chocolate eggs. There are traditional Easter cakes too. ▼

Communion

Communion is a regular part of the church service. It reminds Christians of Jesus' last meal. Everyone has a small amount of bread and wine. Sometimes wafers are used instead of bread, or grape juice instead of wine.

The Jewish Tradition

Yom Kippur

Yom Kippur is the tenth day after the first day of *Rosh Hashanah*, the Jewish New Year. During the days between the two festivals, Jewish people think about the things they have done wrong over the past year. They ask for God's forgiveness so they can start the new year afresh.

A family gathering for the New Year feast. ▼

Yom Kippur is a solemn time. Jewish people go without food to show they want forgiveness for their sins. This means being self-controlled. It helps them to think about others who are less well-off than they are. It is traditional to give to charity at this time.

▲ Jewish people praying. Prayer is very important at Yom Kippur.

SACRED TEXT

'Take away my shame,
Lift my anxiety,
Absolve me of [forgive me]
 my sin
And enable me to pray
 before Thee
With gladness of heart...'

From a *Yom Kippur*
prayer

The day before *Yom Kippur* there is a festive meal. It is a happy, festive occasion, quite different from *Yom Kippur* itself. Everyone wears their best clothes. They light candles and eat a large meal. People don't normally eat spicy or sweet dishes that might be hard to digest. It is important to eat well to prepare for the fast.

Fasting

Jews are commanded in their holy book, the *Torah*, to fast at *Yom Kippur*. Only adults who are fit and healthy may fast, and children fast for part of the day. They can go to the synagogue and focus on their worship. During the long synagogue service, people pray to God and ask him to forgive them for their sins.

These Jews are visiting the holy Wailing Wall in Jerusalem at *Yom Kippur*. ▼

▲ The rabbi blows the *shofar* at the end of the day's prayers.

HAYYIM'S STORY

'I'm 12 and I live in Prague, in the Czech Republic. At *Yom Kippur* we spend the whole day in the synagogue.

'At the end, the rabbi blows a ram's horn called the *shofar*. We go home to break our fast with a tasty meal of cold chicken followed by carrot pudding.'

The Muslim Tradition

Ramadan fast and *Id* feast

Ramadan is the Muslim month of fasting. Muslims do not eat or drink between sunrise and sunset each day. They remember the time when their holy book, the *Qur'an*, was first revealed to the Prophet Muhammad ﷺ.

The fast is one of the Five Pillars of Islam, the five things that all Muslims must do. Muslims believe that fasting brings them closer to Allah. During the month, they spend long periods reciting the *Qur'an*, and think about how they can become better people.

It is traditional to break the fast with some dates. ▼

◀ People put money in the charity box at *Ramadan*.

SACRED TEXT

'...God ordered you to pray during the night, so you prayed, ordered you to fast during the day, so you fasted and obeyed your Lord, so now take your reward.'

From the *Sayings of the Prophet Muhammad* ﷺ

Breaking the fast

Muslims break their fast in the evening with a light snack, such as dates and water. Then they may go to the mosque for sunset prayers. Afterwards, people eat their main meal. It is traditional to have meat, such as chicken, with rice and yoghurt.

A time to be generous

At *Ramadan*, Muslims forgive those who have upset them, and act generously. They give food or money to the mosque to help poorer Muslims to enjoy the festivities after their fast.

Id ul-Fitr

At the end of *Ramadan* comes the feast of *Id ul-Fitr*. People celebrate their strength in fasting, and what they have learnt during the month. They also celebrate Allah's gift of the *Qur'an*.

These children have made beautiful *Id* cards to give away. ▼

AHMED'S STORY

'I live in Morocco. Near the end of *Ramadan*, we celebrate the Night of Power. We remember the first time that the Angel Jibril revealed the *Qur'an* to the Prophet Muhammad ﷺ. We break our fast with dates and water, followed by *harira* soup. (It's made with lentils, chickpeas and vegetables.) Afterwards, we go to the mosque, where people read the *Qur'an* all night long.'

On the day of *Id*, Muslims dress in their best clothes. After prayers at the mosque, families gather for a large celebration meal. Everyone enjoys rich foods, and cakes and sweets. Children receive *Id* presents.

Muslims share a large meal to break the *Ramadan* fast. ▶

The Hindu Tradition

▲ A Hindu priest reading a holy book. Hindus believe it is easier to focus on religious texts while fasting.

Janmashtami

At *Janmashtami*, Hindus celebrate the birth of Krishna. They believe there are many forms of God, and Krishna is a big favourite. Hindus fast at festivals to show devotion to their gods. Fasting helps them to cleanse their minds so they can focus on prayer.

SACRED TEXT

This text warns that Hindus will become like serpents if they don't observe the *Janmashtami* fast.
'...if one neglects to observe the birthday ceremony of Lord Krishna [the person] shall be reborn as a female serpent in a deep forest.'

From the *Bhavishya Purana*

Some Hindus eat nothing at all when they fast. Others
have only milk, yoghurt, fruit and root vegetables.
On the eve of Krishna's birth, they go the temple.
The images of the gods are dressed for the occasion.

These sacred statues of Krishna and his wife
Radha are wearing festive clothes for
Janmashtami. ▼

◀ This picture shows a game played at *Janmashtami*. It is based on the story of how Krishna climbed to the top of a house to steal some butter.

Offerings to baby Krishna

At the temple, people sing holy songs called *bhajans*. When midnight strikes, a sacred statue of baby Krishna is placed in a crib and rocked. People make offerings of his favourite foods – desserts made from dairy products, and sweets. The remaining food is shared out among the worshippers.

The following day, people perform plays about Krishna. Friends and family share a festive meal, and give each other sweets.

A sacred statue of Krishna
playing the flute. ▼

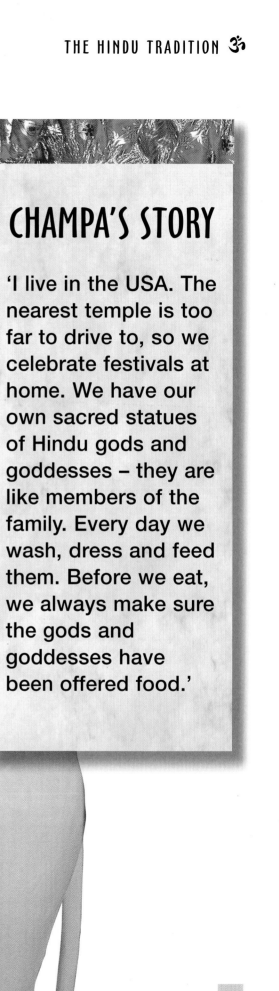

CHAMPA'S STORY

'I live in the USA. The
nearest temple is too
far to drive to, so we
celebrate festivals at
home. We have our
own sacred statues
of Hindu gods and
goddesses – they are
like members of the
family. Every day we
wash, dress and feed
them. Before we eat,
we always make sure
the gods and
goddesses have
been offered food.'

The Sikh Tradition

Fasting

The Sikh religion started in India. Sikhs believe that you can become close to God if you live a good life and serve him well. They do not think that fasting helps your spiritual life.

Guru Nanak, one of the ten Sikh Gurus (teachers), taught that good behaviour is the way to become close to God, rather than fasting. He said: 'Let good conduct be thy [your] fasting.' On festival days, Sikhs do *sewa* – offer service. They give offerings of money or help people in need.

▲ These women are preparing *langar*. All Sikhs take their turn in the kitchen.

Langar

A vital part of Sikh festivals is the shared meal, called *langar*. A group of worshippers prepare the food in the kitchen of the *gurdwara*, their temple. In India, the meal is served throughout the day. In other countries, people eat after the service.

Sharing the same food shows that everybody is equal. It is also an Indian custom to offer food to visitors. Some people may have travelled a long way to reach the *gurdwara*.

SACRED TEXT

'I do not keep the Hindu fast,
nor the Muslim Ramadan
I serve him alone who is my refuge
I serve the one master who is also Allah.
I have broken with the Hindu and the Muslim.
I believe God can be revealed
by observing commandments, righteous living,
and Guru Nanak's morning prayer.'

From *Guru Arjan's Hymn*

Worshippers at the Golden Temple at Amritsar share a *langar* meal. ▶

Guru Nanak's birthday

Gurpurbs are festivals to mark the births and deaths of Gurus. Guru Nanak was the first Guru. His birthday celebrations last three days and *langar* is served throughout. The food is vegetarian so that everybody can eat it.

Prasad, made from flour, butter and sugar, is shared out as part of the service. ▼

In the Punjab, where many Sikhs live, shops and *gurdwaras* are beautifully decorated with lights. People put candles in the windows of their homes.

▲ Sikhs taking the *Guru Granth Sahib* around Southall on the procession.

SANDEEP'S STORY

'I live in Southall, London. At the festival, the *Guru Granth Sahib* is read all the way through – it takes 48 hours! I love going on the procession afterwards. Back at the *gurdwara* my dad listens to the talks through loudspeakers as he helps to cook the *langar*. The food's simple – dhal, rice, roti and vegetable curry. What's special is sharing it with everyone.'

▲ Sikhs taking the *Guru Granth Sahib* around Southall on the procession.

The procession

Sikhs hold a procession with a float carrying their holy book, the *Guru Granth Sahib*. They sing hymns written by Guru Nanak, and children play music and dance. As they walk along, people share out fruit, cakes and sweets.

The Buddhist Tradition

A simple life

Many Buddhists are vegetarian because they do not want to harm animals. They may try to avoid eating foods that cause damage to the environment when they are produced.

The Buddha taught that people should eat neither too much nor too little. Fasting is not encouraged as Buddhists believe that not eating enough makes you unhealthy and confused. Buddhist monks and nuns usually eat only at set times.

Buddhists also believe that drinking alcohol makes it hard for you to behave kindly and wisely. Many Buddhists drink little or no alcohol at all.

Buddhists meditate to help them to become happy and wise. ▶

A woman offers food to Buddhist monks. ▼

Buddhist festivals

Buddhist festivals are joyful occasions. People may go to a temple or monastery to listen to a talk, and to chant and meditate. They offer food to the monks. At most festivals, Buddhists also share out food among the poorest people – even if they are quite poor themselves.

SACRED WRITINGS

This text tells Buddhists they must live sensibly to become wise and happy.

'Whoever lives only for pleasures...will be overthrown...like the wind throws down a weak tree.'

From *The Sayings of the Buddha*

◀ This monk is offering food to peple who are helping to harvest the monastery's crops.

Padmasambhara

Padmasambhara was the founder of Buddhism in Tibet. His birthday is an occasion for meditation and celebration.

In northern India, villagers travel for days to their nearest monastery. Although they are poor themselves, they bring offerings of barley and grain for the monks. They are happy to give away this food. Being generous is an important part of Buddhism.

JOANNE'S STORY

'I live in Paris. On Padmasambhara's birthday we went to the monastery and offered flowers and fruit to the Buddha statue. After listening to a talk and meditating, we went to a party in the park with all our Buddhist friends. There's a huge Buddha statue there. Everybody brought lots of food, which we shared out. All the kids played in the park until really late.'

Worship and food

At the monastery, people offer food to the statue of the Buddha. They meditate in front of the image and chant.

After meditation, they share the food offerings. In India and Tibet, this simple meal may include rice, barley, pulses and yak milk. For people who live in remote places, this is a rare chance to spend time with their friends and families.

Buddhists in a European country prepare a meal for Padmasambhara's birthday celebrations. ▼

Glossary

Allah the Muslim word for God.

Angel Jibril the Angel who visited the Prophet Muhammad ﷺ several times.

chant to say a religious prayer using a few words that are repeated many times.

fast to go without food and drink or without certain foods, often for religious reasons.

gurdwara a Sikh temple.

Guru a Sikh, Hindu or Buddhist teacher.

halal food that Muslims are allowed to eat.

icon a painting or statue of a holy person.

kosher food that Jewish people are allowed to eat.

langar a shared meal eaten in a Sikh temple.

meditate to sit quietly and still to help the person to become calm, happy and wise.

monastery a place where monks live and work together.

offerings food, flowers or other gifts that are offered to a statue of the Buddha to thank him for his teachings.

Orthodox Church the Christian Church in eastern European and North African countries.

priest (in various religions) a person who performs religious ceremonies.

reborn to be born again and have another life.

sins bad actions that break a religious law, such as hurting other people.

yak an animal like a cow, with long horns and long hair.

Books to Read

A Sweet Year: A Taste of the Jewish Holidays by Mark H. Podwal (Doubleday Books for Young Readers, 2003)

A Year of Festivals: Buddhist Festivals Through the Year by Anita Ganeri (Watts, 2003)

A Year of Festivals: Hindu Festivals Throughout the Year by Anita Ganeri (Smart Apple Media, 2004)

Beliefs and Cultures: Buddhist; Christian; Hindu; Jewish; Muslim (Watts, 2003)

Celebrate! Easter by Mike Hirst (Hodder Wayland, 2002)

Festival Tales: Muslim Festivals by Kerena Marchant (Raintree, 2001)

Festivals: Id-Ul-Fitr by Kerena Marchant (Millbrook Press, 1998)

My Buddhist Year; My Hindu Year; My Muslim Year; My Sikh Year; all by Cath Senker (Hodder Wayland, 2003)

My Christian Year; My Jewish Year, both by Cath Senker (Hodder Wayland, 2002)

Our Culture: Buddhist; Hindu; Jewish; Muslim; Sikh (Watts, 2003)

Index

All the numbers in **bold** refer to photographs